I0446723

Introduction

This structured table of contents aims to guide readers through a comprehensive exploration of money psychology, inclusive success, and the broader landscape of wealth creation.

Introduction:

Welcome to "Wealth Mindset Unveiled," a transforming compilation that exceeds standard finance literature, diving into the subtle connection between psychology, wealth generation, and society growth. This book provides a comprehensive investigation of the numerous facets of money, presenting a diverse, informed, and inclusive voice that addresses the unique issues faced by individuals, with a special focus on the reoccurring obstacles confronted by black women in developing successful enterprises.

As we begin on this informative journey, the chapters within "Wealth Mindset Unveiled" build a narrative that encompasses the psychological foundations of wealth, timeless principles, and the keys to inclusive success and happiness. From recognizing the problems faced by female entrepreneurs and founders to addressing the role of chance and risk in wealth management, each chapter contributes to a holistic understanding of the forces at play in the world of finance.

This compilation is more than a guide; it's a call to action for a more egalitarian and educated approach to wealth creation. With an emphasis on different viewpoints, careful money management, and the nurturing of a lasting legacy, "Wealth Mindset Unveiled" challenges you to rethink your relationship with money and empowers you to design a future of inclusive prosperity and fulfillment. Join us on this illuminating journey to explore the actual potential of your wealth mindset.

Chapter 1

Introduction to Money Psychology

In the broad area of personal finance, the basis of wealth isn't exclusively constructed upon dollars and cents but is deeply connected with the human brain. This chapter serves as an entryway into the interesting world of money psychology, seeking to untangle the complexity that shape our ideas, attitudes, and behaviors around money.

Defining Money Psychology:

At its foundation, money psychology studies the fundamental relationship between the human mind and financial decision-making. It comprises a wide spectrum of factors, ranging from emotional responses to financial problems to engrained views about wealth and success. By digging into the subtleties of money psychology, readers obtain a fundamental insight of why individuals make the financial choices they do.

Understanding the delicate dance between the conscious and subconscious mind is vital for anybody seeking financial success. Money, in many respects, becomes a mirror reflecting our deepest fears, wants, and societal conditioning. Acknowledging this relationship opens the way to a more aware and intentional approach to wealth building.

The Impact of Psychological Foundations on Wealth Building:

Our psychological foundations, frequently created in our earliest years, play a key role in molding our financial destinies. Childhood experiences, cultural influences, and society standards establish the lens through which we view money. This chapter goes into the premise that one's money perspective, frequently established in early life, profoundly effects financial decision-making.

For instance, if an individual grows up in an environment where scarcity is the prevailing theme, they might develop a scarcity mindset, leading to fear-based financial decisions. On the opposite side, a person exposed to wealth and positive money tales may build a mindset that invites riches.

Examining the psychological underpinnings of financial actions is analogous to examining the soil in which the seeds of riches are planted. By recognizing these origins, individuals can recognize and fight limiting ideas, cultivating a mindset conducive to wealth generation.

The Interplay Between Beliefs and Attitudes Toward Money:

Beliefs and attitudes are the core of money psychology, influencing how individuals earn, spend, save, and invest. This section analyzes how deeply established views about money can either propel individuals toward financial success or function as impediments to prosperity.

For example, the notion that money is rare and difficult to come by may lead to a dread of taking measured risks or investing. Conversely, a sense in wealth and opportunity may inspire individuals to investigate inventive ways to make income.

By uncovering and altering these ideas, individuals can consciously shift their attitudes about money. This transition creates the framework for a more powerful and intentional approach to financial decision-making.

Navigating Emotional Responses to Financial Situations:

Emotions are significant drivers of human behavior, and when it comes to money, they often take center stage. This section investigates how emotions such as fear, greed, and joy influence financial choices. It provides insights into detecting and managing these emotions to make more sensible and strategic judgments.

For instance, knowing the emotional roots of impulsive spending or hesitation towards investing assists individuals to create coping mechanisms and methods for emotional resilience. By building emotional intelligence in financial topics, readers can cultivate a healthy relationship with money.

In essence, the first chapter provides the basis for a profound exploration into the interesting interplay of psychology and money. By learning the complexities of money psychology, readers begin on a transforming journey towards financial enlightenment, armed with the knowledge to modify their financial destinies.

Chapter 2

Identifying the Psychological Foundations of Wealth

In the complicated tapestry of wealth creation, the threads of our thoughts and attitudes toward money construct the foundation upon which our financial destinies emerge. Chapter 2 digs into the deep field of understanding the psychological roots of wealth, noting that our thinking and views strongly influence our financial success.

Section 1: Unpacking Beliefs and Attitudes Toward Money

Our relationship with money frequently begins in childhood, formed by the values and attitudes common in our families and communities. This section addresses the concept of money scripts, the subconscious assumptions we hold about money that govern our financial habits.

Money Scripts

Origin and Development:

Understanding where our money scripts begin is key to unraveling their impact on our financial lives. Whether inherited from family, affected by societal standards, or modified by personal experiences, these scripts become the lenses through which we view and interact with money.

Common Money Scripts:

Scarcity Mentality: The perception that there is never enough money, leading to persistent anxiety over finances.

Money Avoidance: Averse to dealing with financial concerns, sometimes resulting from negative associations with riches or a fear of corruption.

Money Worship: Equating self-worth with net worth, seeking happiness and validation through material possessions.

Money Status: Associating financial success with personal value, leading to a perpetual pursuit of status symbols.

Impact on Wealth Creation:

Exploring how these scripts impact decision-making, risk-taking, and overall financial behavior sheds light on the psychological barriers that may hinder wealth creation. Strategies for identifying and challenging limiting money scripts are discussed, empowering readers to reshape their financial mindset.

Section 2: Understanding the Role of Mindset in Financial Success

Beyond specific beliefs about money, our mindset, or the lens through which we perceive the world, plays a pivotal role in determining our financial trajectory. This section emphasizes the power of a growth mindset in fostering resilience, adaptability, and a willingness to embrace challenges.

Growth Mindset

Definition and Characteristics:

A growth mindset entails the belief that abilities and intelligence can be developed through dedication and hard work. Contrastingly, a fixed mindset assumes that intelligence and abilities are innate and unchangeable.

Application to Wealth Creation:

Illustrating how a growth mindset contributes to financial success, this section explores real-life examples of individuals who have overcome adversity through persistence, learning from failures, and continuously seeking improvement.

Cultivating a Growth Mindset:

Practical strategies for cultivating a growth mindset are provided, encouraging readers to reframe challenges as opportunities for learning and to embrace a lifelong journey of self-improvement.

The Intersection of Money Scripts and Mindset:

By examining how money scripts and mindset intersect, readers gain a nuanced understanding of their own thought patterns and their impact on financial decisions. The chapter emphasizes the importance of aligning money scripts and mindset with long-term financial goals, fostering a harmonious relationship with wealth creation.

Conclusion:

Chapter 2 concludes by emphasizing the interconnectedness of beliefs, attitudes, and mindset in shaping our financial destinies. Armed with a deeper understanding of the psychological foundations of wealth, readers are better equipped to embark on a transformative journey toward financial success. Recognizing and reshaping limiting beliefs, cultivating a growth mindset, and aligning psychological foundations with long-term goals lay the groundwork for a prosperous and fulfilling financial future.

Chapter 3

Timeless Lessons in Wealth Creation

In the wide tapestry of wealth creation, certain ideas have endured the test of time, providing vital direction to individuals navigating the complex terrain of finance. Chapter 3 of "Wealth Mindset Unveiled" analyzes these eternal ideas, gaining inspiration from historical individuals and extracting universal concepts that transcend generations.

Lesson 1: Learning from Historical Figures:

To comprehend wealth generation, we must first turn our focus to the past. Historical leaders such as Warren Buffett, Benjamin Franklin, and Cleopatra offer insights into the numerous paths one might pursue to accumulate riches. Their stories offer as strong lessons, highlighting the significance of tenacity, strategic thinking, and adaptation.

Warren Buffett, frequently praised as one of the most successful investors of all time, emphasizes the significance of long-term investing and the power of compounding. His systematic approach to financial decisions, built on a profound grasp of businesses and industries, underlines the relevance of knowledge and patience in wealth accumulation.

Benjamin Franklin, a polymath of the 18th century, was not only a Founding Father of the United States but also a wise observer of human behavior. His famous saying, "An investment in knowledge pays the best interest," underscores the timeless importance of education in wealth creation. Franklin's emphasis on continuous learning remains relevant in today's fast-paced and ever-evolving financial landscape.

Cleopatra, the last pharaoh of Ancient Egypt, was not only a charismatic leader but also a shrewd diplomat and economist. Her ability to navigate political complexities and engage in strategic alliances for the economic benefit of her kingdom showcases the interconnectedness of wealth, power, and diplomacy.

Lesson 2: Principles That Stand the Test of Time:

Beyond the stories of individual success, certain principles have consistently proven effective in wealth creation. These principles serve as a compass, guiding individuals through the complexities of financial decision-making.

The principle of diversification, for example, has been advocated by investment experts throughout history. Spreading one's investments across different asset classes helps mitigate risk and enhance long-term returns. Whether in ancient trade routes or modern investment portfolios, the concept of not putting all your eggs in one basket remains a cornerstone of financial wisdom.

Another enduring principle is the importance of discipline and delayed gratification. The ability to resist impulsive financial decisions and prioritize long-term goals over short-term pleasures has been a hallmark of successful wealth builders across cultures and eras.

Lesson 3: Adapting to Change:

While certain principles remain constant, the ability to adapt to changing circumstances is equally crucial. Historical figures and successful entrepreneurs alike have demonstrated the importance of flexibility in the face of economic shifts, technological advancements, and societal changes.

The Industrial Revolution, for instance, reshaped economic landscapes and created new opportunities for wealth creation. Those who embraced innovations and adapted their business models thrived, while those resistant to change faced obsolescence. This lesson resonates strongly in the present era, where rapid technological advancements and the rise of the digital economy demand adaptability from individuals and businesses.

Lesson 4: The Interplay of Ethics and Wealth:

Examining the lives of historical figures also sheds light on the nuanced relationship between ethics and wealth creation. While some amassed fortunes through exploitation and unethical practices, others built legacies grounded in integrity and social responsibility.

The Medicis, a powerful banking family of Renaissance Italy, provides an interesting historical perspective. Their patronage of the arts and contributions to education demonstrate that wealth creation can be a force for cultural and societal advancement. This principle echoes today in the growing movement toward socially responsible investing and businesses that prioritize environmental, social, and governance (ESG) considerations.

Conclusion:

Chapter 3 serves as a journey through time, uncovering the timeless lessons that continue to shape the world of wealth creation. By studying the lives of historical figures and distilling universal principles, readers gain insights into the enduring strategies and values that contribute to lasting financial success. As we navigate the complexities of the contemporary financial landscape, these lessons serve as beacons, guiding us toward a future of informed and sustainable wealth creation.

Chapter 4

Inclusive Success and Happiness

Section 1: Beyond Financial Wealth

Success and happiness are not solely defined by the size of one's bank account. The opening section of this chapter delves into the broader definition of wealth, considering factors such as health, relationships, personal fulfillment, and societal contributions.

1.1 Holistic Definition of Success:

Success goes beyond financial accomplishments; it includes personal growth, emotional well-being, and positive contributions to society. Readers are encouraged to reflect on their own definitions of success, recognizing that fulfillment comes from a balance of various life elements.

1.2 The Importance of Health and Well-being:

Wellness is a cornerstone of true wealth. Mental and physical health contribute significantly to one's ability to enjoy the fruits of financial success. This section explores the symbiotic relationship between health and wealth, urging readers to prioritize self-care.

1.3 Building Meaningful Relationships:

Success is often intertwined with the quality of relationships. The chapter emphasizes the significance of fostering meaningful connections with family, friends, and the community. Building a supportive network is portrayed as a key component of a truly prosperous life.

Section 2: Strategies for Building a Fulfilling Life

Moving beyond theoretical concepts, the second section of the chapter provides practical strategies for readers to enhance their overall well-being and achieve a more fulfilling life.

2.1 Goal Setting and Personal Development:

Readers are guided through the process of setting meaningful goals that align with their values. The chapter emphasizes the importance of continuous learning and personal development as crucial components of a successful and fulfilling life.

2.2 Balancing Professional and Personal Life:

The pursuit of wealth should not come at the expense of personal relationships and well-being. Strategies for achieving a balance between professional and personal life are explored, offering practical tips on time management and setting boundaries.

2.3 Giving Back to Society:

True wealth is magnified when it is used to make a positive impact on the world. The chapter encourages readers to consider how they can contribute to societal well-being, whether through philanthropy, volunteer work, or socially responsible business practices.

Section 3: Case Studies and Success Stories

To bring the concepts to life, this section features case studies and success stories from individuals who have achieved inclusive success and happiness. These stories illustrate the diversity of paths to fulfillment and emphasize that success is a personal journey with no one-size-fits-all formula.

3.1 Case Study: Balancing Business and Well-being

Explore the story of a successful entrepreneur who prioritized health and family alongside building a thriving business. This case study highlights the importance of aligning professional ambitions with personal values.

3.2 Success Story: Making a Difference Through Philanthropy

Discover the journey of an individual who found fulfillment in using their financial success to create positive social change. This success story demonstrates the transformative power of wealth when directed towards altruistic endeavors.

Section 4: Strategies for Navigating Challenges

Recognizing that the path to inclusive success may encounter obstacles, this section equips readers with strategies to navigate challenges and setbacks.

4.1 Resilience and Adaptability:

Success is often accompanied by challenges. Readers are encouraged to develop resilience and adaptability, viewing obstacles as opportunities for growth and learning.

4.2 Overcoming External Expectations:

External pressures and societal expectations can impact one's definition of success. This section explores strategies for overcoming external pressures and staying true to one's authentic aspirations.

Conclusion:

"Inclusive Success and Happiness" concludes by reinforcing the idea that wealth is a multifaceted concept. By broadening our understanding of success and happiness, individuals can cultivate a wealth mindset that not only leads to financial prosperity but also contributes to a more fulfilling and purposeful life. The chapter serves as a guide, inspiring readers to embark on a journey towards inclusive success and happiness, one that encompasses the richness of life in all its dimensions.

Chapter 5

Diversity in Wealth Creation

In the complex tapestry of wealth creation, the importance of diversity cannot be overstated. Chapter 5 of "Wealth Mindset Unveiled" is dedicated to exploring the nuances of diversity in wealth creation, aiming to address the prevalent wealth gap and celebrating success stories from individuals of diverse backgrounds.

Section 1: Addressing the Wealth Gap

The chapter commences with a deep dive into the persistent issue of the wealth gap. It unravels the historical and systemic factors that have contributed to this gap, with a specific focus on the disparities faced by marginalized communities. By dissecting economic policies, educational opportunities, and discriminatory practices, the section paints a comprehensive picture of the challenges that hinder equitable wealth distribution.

Within this section, there is an emphasis on the impact of intersectionality – how race, gender, and socio-economic status intersect to create unique challenges for individuals. This intersectional lens serves as a framework for understanding the layered nature of economic disparities and guides the exploration of solutions to bridge the gap.

Section 2: Celebrating Success Stories

Moving forward, the narrative shifts from challenges to triumphs as the chapter delves into celebrating success stories from diverse backgrounds. Through in-depth interviews and case studies, readers are introduced to individuals who have defied societal norms and overcome adversity to achieve financial success. These stories serve as powerful examples of resilience, determination, and the potential for wealth creation across different demographics.

One compelling aspect of this section is the spotlight on cultural nuances and unique strategies employed by individuals from various backgrounds. By showcasing a spectrum of experiences, the chapter strives to dismantle stereotypes and illustrate that there is no one-size-fits-all approach to wealth creation. Instead, it encourages readers to draw inspiration from a variety of pathways to success.

Section 3: The Role of Cultural Competency in Wealth Building

To further enrich the discussion, the chapter explores the concept of cultural competency in the context of wealth building. It recognizes that financial systems and opportunities are often structured without consideration for diverse cultural perspectives. By fostering an understanding of different cultural values, practices, and approaches to money, readers are equipped with insights that can inform more inclusive financial strategies.

This section emphasizes the importance of financial institutions and professionals adopting culturally competent practices. It advocates for tailored financial education programs that acknowledge and incorporate the diversity of experiences, ultimately paving the way for a more inclusive and accessible financial landscape.

Section 4: Collaborative Strategies for Change

The chapter culminates with a call to action, proposing collaborative strategies for addressing the wealth gap and promoting diversity in wealth creation. It explores the role of governments, businesses, and communities in creating an environment that fosters equitable opportunities. This section also touches on the significance of mentorship and community support networks in empowering individuals from underrepresented backgrounds to navigate the complexities of wealth creation.

Through an exploration of both challenges and successes, Chapter 5 aims to inspire readers to engage in conversations about diversity in wealth creation. By understanding the intricacies of the wealth gap and celebrating diverse success stories, the chapter encourages a paradigm shift towards more inclusive financial practices and a future where wealth creation is not bound by societal biases.

Chapter 6:
Challenges Faced by Female Entrepreneurs

In the ever-evolving landscape of entrepreneurship, women have been breaking barriers and making significant strides. However, the journey for female entrepreneurs is often riddled with unique challenges that require resilience, innovation, and a steadfast mindset. Chapter 6 explores the multifaceted challenges faced by female entrepreneurs, aiming to shed light on the disparities and highlight strategies for overcoming gender bias in business.

Section 1: Navigating Entrepreneurship as a Woman

The entrepreneurial path for women is often strewn with obstacles that differ from those faced by their male counterparts. From securing funding to establishing credibility, female entrepreneurs grapple with societal expectations and gender biases. This section delves into the nuanced experiences of women navigating the business world, offering insights into the hurdles they face and the strategies employed to overcome them.

1.1 Gender Bias in Funding:

One of the primary challenges faced by female entrepreneurs is the persistent gender bias in funding. Studies consistently show that women-led startups receive a disproportionately small share of venture capital. This subsection explores the systemic issues contributing to this bias and discusses initiatives aimed at fostering a more equitable investment landscape.

1.2 Building Credibility in a Male-Dominated Environment:

Establishing credibility is crucial for any entrepreneur, but for women, it can be a more arduous task in male-dominated industries. From overcoming stereotypes to breaking through the glass ceiling, female entrepreneurs often find themselves having to prove their competence more rigorously. This section highlights the experiences of successful women who have navigated these challenges and emerged as leaders in their fields.

Section 2: Overcoming Gender Bias in Business

While challenges persist, many female entrepreneurs have successfully overcome gender bias to build thriving businesses. This section explores inspirational stories and strategies employed by women who have shattered the glass ceiling, providing valuable lessons for aspiring female entrepreneurs.

2.1 Mentorship and Networking:

Building a strong network and seeking mentorship are key strategies for overcoming gender bias. Female entrepreneurs often benefit from the guidance of mentors who have navigated similar challenges. This subsection explores the importance of mentorship programs and networks designed to support women in entrepreneurship.

2.2 Advocacy and Policy Initiatives:

Advocacy plays a crucial role in challenging and dismantling gender bias in business. This section discusses the impact of policy initiatives aimed at promoting diversity and inclusion in entrepreneurship. It highlights successful campaigns and legislative measures that have contributed to a more supportive environment for female entrepreneurs.

2.3 Fostering a Culture of Inclusion:

Creating a culture of inclusion within organizations and industries is essential for breaking down gender barriers. This subsection explores how companies and institutions can actively work towards fostering an environment that values diversity, ensuring that female entrepreneurs are given equal opportunities to thrive.

Conclusion:

Chapter 6 concludes by emphasizing the resilience and achievements of female entrepreneurs, celebrating the progress that has been made, and highlighting the ongoing work needed to create a more inclusive entrepreneurial landscape. By addressing the unique challenges faced by women in business, this chapter aims to inspire readers to champion diversity and contribute to a future where entrepreneurship knows no gender boundaries.

Chapter 7

The Female Founder's Journey

The entrepreneurial landscape is evolving, and women are increasingly making their mark as founders and leaders of successful businesses. However, the journey for female entrepreneurs, particularly women of color, is often characterized by unique challenges and triumphs. In this chapter, we explore the inspiring stories of female founders, highlighting the hurdles they faced and the invaluable lessons learned along the way.

Section 1: Navigating Challenges

To truly understand the female founder's journey, it's crucial to acknowledge the obstacles they encounter. Gender bias, limited access to capital, and societal expectations are among the many hurdles that women face when establishing and growing their ventures. This section aims to shed light on the resilience and determination exhibited by female entrepreneurs in overcoming these challenges.

1.1 Overcoming Gender Bias

Female entrepreneurs often contend with gender bias, both overt and subtle, in various aspects of their professional lives. This includes biases in networking opportunities, investment decisions, and even perceptions of leadership. Real-life anecdotes from successful female founders will be shared to illustrate how they navigated and challenged these biases, paving the way for themselves and future generations.

1.2 Limited Access to Capital

Access to capital remains a significant barrier for women looking to start and scale their businesses. Statistics reveal a stark contrast in funding received by male and female-led enterprises. This section explores the impact of limited access to capital on female founders and shares stories of resourcefulness and creativity in securing funding.

1.3 Societal Expectations

Societal expectations and stereotypes about gender roles can influence how female founders are perceived and treated in the business world. This section will delve into the ways in which societal expectations shape the entrepreneurial journey for women, and how successful female founders have challenged these norms to carve out their own paths.

Section 2: Success Stories

Despite the challenges, numerous female founders have not only succeeded but thrived in their respective industries. This section aims to celebrate their achievements, providing a platform for their stories to inspire and motivate aspiring entrepreneurs. Each success story will be accompanied by an analysis of the key factors that contributed to their triumphs.

2.1 Case Study: [Founder A] - Breaking Barriers in Tech

Highlighting the journey of a female founder who excelled in the male-dominated tech industry. From founding her startup to navigating the challenges of raising capital, this case study explores the strategies employed to break through barriers and create a successful enterprise.

2.2 Case Study: [Founder B] - Pioneering Social Impact

Examining the story of a female founder who prioritized social impact in her business model. This case study will showcase how a commitment to purpose-driven entrepreneurship can lead to both financial success and positive societal change.

2.3 Case Study: [Founder C] - Empowering Other Women

Exploring the journey of a female founder who not only built a successful business but also dedicated her efforts to empower and uplift other women in the entrepreneurial space. This case study delves into the importance of mentorship and community building among female founders.

Section 3: Lessons Learned and Shared Wisdom

In this section, the focus shifts to the insights gained by female founders throughout their entrepreneurial journeys. Their wisdom and advice become invaluable resources for aspiring entrepreneurs, offering guidance on resilience, leadership, and the importance of fostering a supportive ecosystem.

3.1 Resilience in the Face of Adversity

Female founders often develop a remarkable level of resilience through their experiences. This section explores the various forms of resilience exhibited by successful women entrepreneurs, emphasizing how these qualities contribute to long-term success.

3.2 Leadership Styles and Strategies

Examining the diverse leadership styles employed by female founders, this section emphasizes the importance of authentic leadership. Successful female entrepreneurs bring unique perspectives and approaches to leadership, challenging traditional norms and fostering inclusive work environments.

3.3 Building a Supportive Ecosystem

Female founders frequently highlight the significance of a supportive network in their success. This section explores how building and nurturing such networks—comprising mentors, peers, and allies—can be a game-changer for women in entrepreneurship.

Conclusion:

"The Female Founder's Journey" is a testament to the resilience, innovation, and leadership exhibited by women in the entrepreneurial space. By understanding and celebrating their experiences, we not only honor their achievements but also pave the way for a more inclusive and supportive future for all aspiring entrepreneurs, irrespective of gender or background. The stories shared in this chapter serve as beacons of inspiration, encouraging readers to embrace their entrepreneurial aspirations with confidence and determination.

Chapter 8

Investing with a Purpose

In the ever-evolving landscape of wealth creation, investing is a cornerstone of financial success. However, "Investing with a Purpose" goes beyond traditional investment strategies; it explores the intersection of investing and social impact, advocating for a purpose-driven approach to wealth management. This chapter seeks to empower readers to align their financial goals with broader societal benefits, fostering a sense of responsibility and creating positive change through investment choices.

Understanding Impact Investing:

Impact investing is a philosophy that seeks to generate positive and measurable social or environmental impact alongside financial returns. In recent years, there has been a growing awareness of the role investments can play in addressing societal challenges. Investors are increasingly considering the broader implications of their financial decisions, looking beyond profit margins to assess how their investments contribute to a better world.

Defining Impact:

Impact, in the context of investing, refers to the positive change or contribution that an investment makes to society or the environment.
The impact can be measured in various ways, such as social metrics, environmental sustainability, or community development.

Socially Responsible Investing (SRI):

SRI involves selecting investments based on ethical, social, and environmental criteria. Investors may choose to support companies that align with their values, avoiding those with practices deemed harmful.

Case Studies in Purposeful Investing:

To illustrate the concept of investing with a purpose, this chapter features real-world case studies of individuals and organizations that have successfully integrated impact investing into their financial strategies.

Microfinance Initiatives:

Explore how investing in microfinance institutions has empowered entrepreneurs in underserved communities.
Highlight success stories of individuals who have lifted themselves out of poverty through access to microcredit.

Renewable Energy Investments:

Showcase the impact of investing in renewable energy projects.
Discuss the role of investors in accelerating the transition to a more sustainable and environmentally friendly energy sector.

Community Development Funds:

Examine the positive effects of investing in community development funds.
Illustrate how these funds contribute to infrastructure, education, and healthcare in disadvantaged areas.

Balancing Financial Returns and Impact:

One of the key challenges in impact investing is finding the right balance between financial returns and societal impact. This section of the chapter delves into strategies for achieving a harmonious blend of profitability and purpose.

Risk Management in Impact Investing:

Discuss the potential risks associated with impact investing.
Provide insights into risk mitigation strategies to ensure a sustainable and responsible investment portfolio.

Measuring Impact:

Explore the methodologies and tools available for measuring the social and environmental impact of investments.
Highlight the importance of transparent reporting and accountability in impact measurement.

Long-Term Perspective:

Emphasize the long-term benefits of impact investing.
Showcase how patient capital can lead to sustainable positive change over time.

Empowering Individuals to Invest with Purpose:

To make impact investing accessible to a broader audience, this section of the chapter provides practical guidance for individuals looking to align their investments with their values.

Identifying Personal Values:

Guide readers through a self-assessment to identify their core values and priorities.
Help readers understand how their values can shape their investment choices.

Researching Impact Opportunities:

Provide resources and tools for researching impact investment opportunities.
Highlight platforms that connect investors with socially responsible investment options.

Collaborative Investing:

Explore the concept of collaborative or pooled impact investing.
Showcase the power of collective action in driving positive change through investments.

Conclusion:

"Investing with a Purpose" encourages readers to view their investment portfolios as powerful tools for change. By aligning financial goals with broader societal benefits, individuals can contribute to a more equitable and sustainable world. This chapter aims to inspire a new generation of investors who recognize the transformative potential of purposeful investing, transcending the traditional boundaries of wealth creation to make a positive impact on the world.

Chapter 9

Acknowledging Achievements

In the pursuit of wealth and success, the acknowledgment of one's achievements plays a pivotal role. Chapter 9 of "Wealth Mindset Unveiled" is dedicated to understanding the importance of acknowledging accomplishments, celebrating milestones, and recognizing the efforts that contribute to an individual's financial journey.

The Power of Acknowledgment:

Acknowledgment is a fundamental human need that extends beyond mere recognition; it is about validating one's efforts and accomplishments. In the context of wealth creation, acknowledgment becomes a powerful motivator, driving individuals to reach their financial goals. This chapter explores the psychological impact of acknowledgment and how it shapes the mindset of those on the path to financial success.

1. Recognition as a Motivational Tool:

Case Studies: Share success stories of individuals who achieved financial milestones and how acknowledgment played a role in motivating them.
Expert Insights: Include insights from psychologists and motivational speakers on the impact of acknowledgment on human behavior.

Recognition is not just a formality; it serves as a motivational tool. When individuals feel seen and appreciated for their efforts, it boosts their confidence and encourages them to strive for even greater accomplishments. By delving into real-life examples and expert opinions, readers gain a deeper understanding of the psychological dynamics at play.

2. Cultivating a Positive Mindset:

Mindset Shift Strategies: Provide practical strategies for cultivating a positive mindset through self-acknowledgment and celebrating small wins.

The Role of Positive Reinforcement: Explore how acknowledgment contributes to the development of a growth mindset, essential for long-term success.

Acknowledgment goes beyond external validation; it fosters a positive internal dialogue. This section delves into the ways in which individuals can actively cultivate a positive mindset by acknowledging their achievements. It emphasizes the importance of self-acknowledgment in the face of challenges and setbacks.

Celebrating Milestones:

Financial journeys are marked by various milestones, both big and small. Chapter 9 explores the significance of celebrating these milestones, offering a roadmap for readers to appreciate their progress and maintain enthusiasm throughout their wealth-building endeavors.

1. Milestones as Building Blocks:

Mapping Financial Milestones: Provide a guide on setting realistic financial milestones and breaking down larger goals into manageable steps.

The Cumulative Effect: Discuss how acknowledging and celebrating small victories can have a cumulative effect on overall well-being and success.

Acknowledging achievements is not just reserved for major accomplishments; it starts with recognizing the significance of small victories. By breaking down financial goals into milestones, individuals can celebrate their progress, reinforcing positive habits and behaviors.

2. Rituals of Celebration:

Personal Celebrations: Encourage readers to develop personal rituals for celebrating achievements.

Community Celebrations: Explore the importance of celebrating within communities, whether that be family, friends, or professional networks.

Rituals of celebration create a sense of accomplishment and contribute to the emotional aspect of financial success. Whether it's a personal ritual or a communal celebration, the chapter highlights the various ways individuals can infuse joy into their financial journeys.

The Role of Acknowledgment in Inclusive Success:

This section of the chapter delves into the importance of acknowledgment in fostering inclusive success. It specifically addresses the challenges faced by black women in the business and financial world, emphasizing the need for acknowledgment as a tool for empowerment and equity.

1. Acknowledgment as Empowerment:

Intersectionality in Wealth Building: Explore how acknowledgment becomes a tool for empowerment, especially for individuals facing intersectional challenges.
Stories of Resilience: Share stories of black women who have overcome obstacles, emphasizing the role acknowledgment played in their success.
Acknowledgment becomes a potent force in breaking down barriers and promoting inclusivity. By acknowledging the unique challenges faced by black women, the chapter advocates for a more supportive and empowering environment.

2. Equity and Acknowledgment:

Addressing Disparities: Discuss how acknowledgment can be a means to address and rectify systemic disparities in access to opportunities.
Corporate Responsibility: Explore the role of corporations and institutions in acknowledging and addressing the challenges faced by underrepresented groups.
Acknowledgment is not just an individual responsibility; it extends to the collective. This section examines how acknowledgment can be a catalyst for systemic change, promoting equity and inclusivity on a larger scale.

Implementing Acknowledgment Strategies:
The final part of the chapter provides actionable strategies for implementing acknowledgment in one's life and within the broader community. It serves as a practical guide, empowering readers to actively incorporate acknowledgment into their wealth-building journeys.

1. Self-Acknowledgment Practices:
Gratitude Journals: Encourage the use of gratitude journals as a tool for self-acknowledgment.
Reflection Exercises: Provide guided reflection exercises to help readers recognize and appreciate their achievements.
Acknowledgment begins with oneself. By fostering self-acknowledgment practices, individuals can build a foundation for sustained motivation and resilience.

2. Building Inclusive Communities:
Networking Events: Highlight the importance of networking events that celebrate diversity and inclusion.
Mentorship Programs: Explore how mentorship programs can incorporate acknowledgment as a key element.
The chapter concludes by emphasizing the role of inclusive communities in creating a supportive environment. By actively acknowledging the achievements of diverse individuals, communities contribute to the overall well-being and success of their members.

In essence, Chapter 9 of "Wealth Mindset Unveiled" provides readers with a comprehensive understanding of the psychological impact of acknowledgment on wealth creation. By exploring the motivational power of recognition, the significance of celebrating milestones, and the role of acknowledgment in fostering inclusive success, the chapter serves as a guide for individuals on their journey to financial empowerment and fulfillment.

Chapter 10

Chance and Risk in Wealth Management

The threads of chance and risk are closely woven together in the complicated tapestry of wealth management, impacting financial decisions and consequences. The tenth chapter of "Wealth Mindset Unveiled" delves into the delicate balance between seizing chances and handling uncertainties, providing readers with insights into the dynamic interplay of chance and risk in the quest of financial success.

Understanding Chance:

Chance, often synonymous with opportunity, is a force that can shape financial destinies in unexpected ways. It manifests in the form of unforeseen events, market fluctuations, and serendipitous moments that can either propel individuals toward wealth or introduce challenges that demand resilience and adaptability.

Opportunities in the Unknown:

Examining how embracing uncertainty can lead to opportunities.
Real-life stories of individuals who capitalized on unexpected chances to build wealth.

Market Dynamics and Timing:

Insight into the volatile nature of financial markets.
Strategies for recognizing and seizing favorable market conditions.

The Role of Networking and Relationships:

How personal and professional connections can create unexpected opportunities.
Building a network that enhances the likelihood of encountering beneficial chances.

Understanding Risk:

On the flip side, risk is an inherent aspect of wealth management that requires careful consideration and strategic planning. While chance presents opportunities, risk introduces the potential for loss and setbacks.

Types of Financial Risks:

Market risk, credit risk, and operational risk explained.
Diversification as a risk management strategy.

Psychology of Risk-Taking:

Analyzing individual risk tolerance and risk aversion.
How psychological factors influence decision-making in the face of risk.

Balancing Risk and Reward:

Strategies for optimizing risk-return profiles.
The concept of a risk-reward spectrum and finding the right balance.

Case Studies:

To provide a practical understanding of chance and risk, this chapter incorporates case studies featuring individuals from diverse backgrounds and industries. These case studies will illustrate real-world scenarios where individuals navigated uncertainties, took calculated risks, and reaped rewards, offering readers valuable lessons and insights.

The Entrepreneurial Gamble:

Examining how entrepreneurs balance risk and reward in their ventures.
Stories of successful entrepreneurs who took strategic risks to achieve financial success.

Investment Strategies in Dynamic Markets:

How seasoned investors approach risk in ever-changing markets.
Case studies highlighting investment decisions that paid off despite market fluctuations.

Navigating Career Risks:

Exploring how career choices and changes involve inherent risks.
Stories of professionals who embraced career risks and achieved financial prosperity.

Strategies for Mitigating Risk:

Recognizing that risk is an inevitable part of wealth management, this chapter offers
practical strategies for mitigating and managing risks effectively.

Diversification and Asset Allocation:

The importance of a well-diversified portfolio in reducing risk.
Guidelines for strategic asset allocation based on individual financial goals and risk
tolerance.

Risk Management Tools and Techniques:

Introduction to risk management tools, such as insurance and hedging.
How these tools can be employed to minimize the impact of potential financial losses.

Continuous Learning and Adaptability:

The role of education and staying informed in risk management.
How adaptability and a willingness to learn can enhance financial resilience.

Conclusion:

Chapter 10 concludes by emphasizing that an informed and calculated approach to chance and risk is essential for building sustainable wealth. By understanding the dynamics of opportunity and uncertainty, readers can navigate the complexities of wealth management with confidence, resilience, and a strategic mindset. Ultimately, the chapter seeks to empower individuals to embrace chance, manage risk effectively, and embark on a path to financial success.

Chapter 11

Limited Access to Capital for Women

In the landscape of wealth creation, access to capital is a fundamental element that can either propel or impede one's financial journey. Unfortunately, for many women, particularly black women, limited access to capital remains a pervasive challenge. This chapter aims to dissect the intricacies of this issue, shedding light on the systemic barriers and proposing strategies for dismantling them.

Understanding the Disparities:

The gender gap in access to capital is a multifaceted problem rooted in historical, social, and economic factors. Black women entrepreneurs often face intersecting challenges that compound the difficulties of securing funding. Discrimination, bias, and stereotypes play a significant role in limiting opportunities for financial support. Studies reveal that women-led businesses receive only a fraction of the venture capital that male-led businesses do, and this gap is even wider for women of color.

The Intersectionality of Challenges:

Black women, as both entrepreneurs and investors, find themselves navigating a complex intersection of challenges. Stereotypes about the capabilities of women, coupled with racial biases, create a unique set of hurdles that hinder financial progress. Moreover, limited networks and mentorship opportunities contribute to a lack of exposure, making it difficult for black women to access crucial funding channels.

Systemic Barriers:

The systemic barriers to capital access for black women are deeply embedded in financial institutions and traditional funding mechanisms. The criteria for loan approvals and investment decisions often reflect biased standards that fail to consider the diverse range of businesses led by women of color. The lack of representation in decision-making positions further exacerbates these challenges.

Alternative Funding Solutions:

Recognizing the limitations of traditional financing, black women entrepreneurs are increasingly exploring alternative funding solutions. Crowdfunding platforms, community-based financing, and impact investing are emerging as viable options. These avenues not only provide financial support but also foster a sense of community and empowerment.

Success Stories:

Amidst the challenges, there are inspiring success stories of black women who have overcome the odds and secured funding for their ventures. These stories serve as beacons of hope and demonstrate the resilience and ingenuity of black women entrepreneurs. Highlighting these successes is crucial for challenging stereotypes and showcasing the untapped potential within this demographic.

Advocacy for Change:

Addressing the issue of limited access to capital for black women requires a concerted effort from various stakeholders. Advocacy groups, policymakers, financial institutions, and the broader business community all have roles to play. Initiatives that promote diversity and inclusion in entrepreneurship and investment, as well as policy reforms that address discriminatory lending practices, are essential for creating a more equitable financial landscape.

Mentorship and Networking:

Building robust networks and mentorship programs specifically tailored for black women entrepreneurs can significantly impact their access to capital. Connecting with experienced mentors who understand the unique challenges faced by women of color in business can provide invaluable guidance and open doors to funding opportunities.

Education and Empowerment:

Financial literacy and empowerment programs targeted at black women can contribute to breaking the cycle of limited access to capital. By equipping women with the knowledge and skills needed to navigate the financial landscape, these programs empower them to advocate for themselves and make informed decisions about their businesses.

Conclusion:

Chapter 11 sheds light on the pressing issue of limited access to capital for black women, emphasizing the need for a comprehensive and intersectional approach to address this challenge. By understanding the systemic barriers, exploring alternative funding solutions, celebrating success stories, advocating for change, and fostering mentorship and education, we can work towards a future where all individuals, regardless of gender or race, have equal opportunities to thrive in the world of finance.

Chapter 12

Money-Spending Behaviors and Views

Money-spending behaviors and views play a pivotal role in an individual's financial well-being. In this chapter, we delve deep into the intricate dynamics of how people spend money, the psychological factors that influence spending habits, and the importance of shaping a healthy relationship with money. Understanding these aspects is crucial for achieving financial stability and fostering a mindset conducive to wealth creation.

Section 1: Exploring Individual Spending Habits

1.1 Personal Finance and Individual Choices

The chapter begins by acknowledging the diversity of spending habits among individuals. It recognizes that personal finance is deeply personal, influenced by cultural, social, and individual factors. Some people may be natural savers, while others are more inclined towards spending. By understanding and respecting these differences, readers can gain insights into their own spending patterns and those of others.

1.2 The Influence of Societal Norms

Societal norms and expectations often shape how individuals approach spending. From conspicuous consumption to the minimalist movement, society plays a significant role in dictating what is considered "normal" or "acceptable" when it comes to spending money. This section explores the impact of societal pressures on spending choices and encourages readers to critically evaluate these influences.

1.3 Emotional Spending

Emotions are powerful drivers of spending behavior. Whether it's retail therapy to cope with stress or impulse purchases fueled by excitement, understanding the emotional aspect of spending is essential. The chapter delves into the psychology behind emotional spending, offering practical tips for recognizing and managing these impulses.

Section 2: Shaping Healthy Money Perspectives

2.1 Building Financial Awareness

To foster healthy money-spending behaviors, individuals need to cultivate financial awareness. This involves understanding one's financial situation, setting realistic goals, and creating a budget. The chapter provides practical exercises and tools to help readers assess their financial awareness and take proactive steps towards building a solid financial foundation.

2.2 The Role of Financial Education

Financial education is a key component of shaping healthy money perspectives. Unfortunately, formal education often falls short in providing individuals with the necessary financial literacy skills. This section advocates for the integration of financial education into school curricula and emphasizes the importance of ongoing learning throughout adulthood.

2.3 Overcoming the Fear of Budgeting

Many individuals find the idea of budgeting intimidating or restrictive. This section addresses common fears associated with budgeting and presents it as a empowering tool rather than a constraint. By reframing budgeting as a means to achieve financial goals and aspirations, readers can overcome their reservations and take control of their finances.

Section 3: Practical Strategies for Responsible Spending

3.1 Creating a Purposeful Spending Plan

A purposeful spending plan involves aligning one's spending habits with personal values and long-term goals. This section guides readers through the process of creating a spending plan that reflects their priorities, ensuring that money is allocated to what truly matters to them.

3.2 The Art of Delayed Gratification

Delayed gratification is a fundamental principle in responsible money management. This section explores the psychological benefits of delaying immediate desires for long-term rewards. Strategies such as setting financial milestones and practicing mindful spending are discussed to help readers cultivate the patience necessary for delayed gratification.

3.3 Navigating Peer Pressure and Consumer Culture

Peer pressure and consumer culture can exert significant influence on spending choices. This section provides strategies for resisting external pressures and making decisions that align with individual financial goals. It emphasizes the importance of cultivating financial resilience in the face of societal expectations.

Conclusion:

Chapter 12 concludes by emphasizing that money-spending behaviors are not just about financial transactions but are deeply rooted in psychology. By understanding the factors that influence spending habits and adopting practical strategies for responsible spending, readers can pave the way for financial well-being and long-term wealth creation. Shaping a healthy money mindset is a continuous journey, and this chapter serves as a comprehensive guide for individuals seeking to take control of their financial destinies.

Chapter 13

Childhood Psychology and Financial Education

In the journey toward financial empowerment, the role of childhood psychology and early financial education cannot be overstated. Chapter 13 of "Wealth Mindset Unveiled" is dedicated to exploring the intricate relationship between childhood psychology and financial literacy. It delves into the impact of early experiences on money management skills, emphasizing the need for a comprehensive and inclusive approach to financial education.

Understanding the Foundations:

Childhood experiences play a pivotal role in shaping an individual's relationship with money. The family, as the primary socializing agent, significantly influences a child's attitudes, beliefs, and behaviors related to finances. The chapter begins by unraveling the psychological foundations laid during childhood and how they contribute to the development of financial habits later in life.

The Role of Parents and Caregivers:

Examining the influence of parental attitudes toward money on children. Strategies for fostering a healthy and positive money mindset at home. The importance of open communication about finances within families.

Early Money Experiences:

Exploring the impact of a child's first encounters with money. How positive or negative experiences can shape future financial behaviors. Introducing age-appropriate financial concepts to children.

Building a Foundation for Financial Literacy:

This section of the chapter focuses on practical steps and strategies to integrate financial education into childhood development. It emphasizes the need for a structured and age-appropriate approach to ensure that children develop a strong foundation in financial literacy.

Incorporating Financial Education into School Curriculum:

Advocating for the inclusion of financial literacy in school curricula.
Collaborating with educators to design engaging and effective financial education programs.
Highlighting successful examples of schools that have implemented comprehensive financial literacy initiatives.

Interactive Learning and Play:

The role of games and interactive activities in teaching financial concepts to children.
Designing age-appropriate games that promote financial literacy.
Showcasing successful educational programs that use play-based learning for financial education.

Digital Tools and Resources:

Leveraging technology to enhance financial education for children.
Recommending age-appropriate apps and online resources for financial learning.
Addressing concerns and considerations related to children's use of digital financial tools.

Empowering Parents and Caregivers:

Recognizing the pivotal role of parents and caregivers in the financial education of children, this section provides guidance and resources to empower adults in fostering a positive and informed money mindset in their children.

Parental Involvement in Financial Education:

Encouraging parents to actively participate in their children's financial education.
Offering workshops and resources for parents to enhance their own financial literacy.
Creating a supportive community for parents to share experiences and best practices.

Addressing Socioeconomic Disparities:

Recognizing the challenges faced by families with limited financial resources.
Implementing targeted programs to address socioeconomic disparities in financial education.
Collaborating with community organizations to provide accessible resources for all families.

Conclusion:

Chapter 13 concludes by emphasizing the long-term impact of childhood psychology on financial well-being. It underscores the importance of a collective effort from families, schools, and communities to instill a positive and inclusive money mindset in the next generation. By recognizing the significance of childhood experiences and investing in comprehensive financial education, society can pave the way for a future where individuals are empowered to navigate the complexities of finance with confidence and competence. "Wealth Mindset Unveiled" encourages readers to reflect on their own childhood experiences and consider how they can contribute to creating a more financially literate and empowered society.

Chapter 14

Encouraging Financial Empowerment

Financial empowerment is a journey that transcends traditional wealth-building concepts. It involves equipping individuals with the knowledge, skills, and mindset needed to take control of their financial destinies. In this chapter, we will delve into the multifaceted aspects of financial empowerment, exploring strategies to foster a culture of financial independence and inclusivity.

The Foundations of Financial Empowerment

Financial empowerment goes beyond accumulating wealth; it encompasses the ability to make informed financial decisions that align with one's goals and values. It starts with education, understanding the principles of budgeting, saving, investing, and managing debt. For many, financial literacy is a gateway to empowerment. Therefore, initiatives aimed at promoting financial education should be accessible to people of all backgrounds.

Breaking Down Barriers: Inclusive Financial Education

To encourage financial empowerment, it is imperative to break down barriers to access quality financial education. This includes addressing disparities in educational resources and tailoring programs to resonate with diverse audiences. Educational initiatives should recognize the unique challenges faced by groups such as black women in their pursuit of financial success, offering targeted content that addresses their specific needs and experiences.

Technology as an Enabler of Financial Inclusivity

In the digital age, technology has the power to democratize access to financial information and services. Mobile apps, online courses, and interactive platforms can provide a bridge to financial literacy, making it more accessible to individuals who may have limited resources or face geographical constraints. Embracing technology in financial education ensures a wider reach and fosters inclusivity.

Mentorship and Role Models

The importance of mentorship cannot be overstated in the journey towards financial empowerment. Creating mentorship programs that connect experienced individuals with those seeking guidance can provide valuable insights and support. For black women entrepreneurs and professionals, having access to mentors who have navigated similar challenges can be particularly empowering, offering not only practical advice but also emotional support.

Community Engagement and Support Networks

Building a sense of community is crucial in fostering financial empowerment. Establishing support networks that facilitate open discussions about financial challenges, successes, and strategies can create a supportive environment. For black women confronting unique obstacles, such communities become a source of strength, inspiration, and shared wisdom. Initiatives that encourage the formation of such networks contribute to a more inclusive financial landscape.

Advocacy for Policy Changes

Achieving widespread financial empowerment requires systemic changes. Advocacy for policy changes that address gender and racial disparities in access to capital, education, and opportunities is essential. By working towards creating an environment that values diversity and inclusivity, we pave the way for a more equitable financial future.

Cultivating a Mindset of Financial Independence

Empowering individuals involves cultivating a mindset of financial independence. This includes instilling confidence in one's ability to make sound financial decisions, irrespective of background or gender. Educational programs that focus on building financial confidence and resilience contribute to a culture where individuals feel empowered to take charge of their financial well-being.

Tailoring Strategies for Different Demographics

Recognizing the unique challenges faced by various demographics is crucial in developing effective strategies for financial empowerment. Tailoring programs to address the specific needs of black women, entrepreneurs, founders, and investors ensures that the initiatives are relevant and impactful. By acknowledging the diversity of experiences, we can create inclusive solutions that resonate with a broad audience.

Encouraging Entrepreneurship and Investment

Financial empowerment extends to fostering entrepreneurship and investment opportunities. Initiatives that provide access to capital, mentorship, and networking for underrepresented groups can catalyze economic growth and bridge the wealth gap. Encouraging and supporting entrepreneurship among black women requires a concerted effort to remove barriers and create an ecosystem conducive to business success.

Integrating Financial Education into Formal Curriculum

To create lasting change, financial education should be integrated into formal education systems. By incorporating financial literacy into school curricula, we can equip future generations with the skills needed for responsible financial management. This approach not only addresses the root of financial illiteracy but also promotes a cultural shift towards valuing financial education as an essential life skill.

Measuring Success and Impact

Assessing the success of financial empowerment initiatives involves tracking both quantitative and qualitative metrics. Quantitative measures may include improvements in financial literacy rates, increased savings, and higher rates of entrepreneurship among underrepresented groups. Qualitative measures could encompass improved confidence in financial decision-making and a sense of empowerment within communities.

Conclusion

Chapter 14 of "Wealth Mindset Unveiled" underscores the importance of financial empowerment as a catalyst for positive change. By exploring the multifaceted aspects of financial education, mentorship, community engagement, and systemic advocacy, we aim to provide readers with actionable insights to foster a culture of inclusivity, diversity, and financial independence. The journey towards wealth creation should be accessible to all, and through empowering individuals with the tools and knowledge they need, we can collectively build a more equitable and prosperous future.

Chapter 15

Creating a Future of Inclusive Wealth

An attitude of wealth With our future vision unveiled, we set out to imagine and build a society in which money represents inclusivity, empowerment, and shared prosperity rather than only being a gauge of financial success. As a call to action, this chapter provides methods and perspectives for bringing about constructive change in the areas of financial systems, wealth creation, and public perceptions of money.

1. Reflecting on the Path Traveled:

It's important to consider the most important lessons from our investigation of money psychology and inclusive success before we get started defining the future. The psychological underpinnings of wealth, timeless teachings, and many success stories that have been discussed throughout the book are urged to be reviewed by readers. It is possible to take a proactive and knowledgeable attitude to the future by thinking back on past lessons.

2. Redefining Success Beyond Numbers:

The chapter begins by challenging conventional notions of success tied solely to monetary wealth. It encourages readers to redefine success by incorporating elements of personal fulfillment, community impact, and holistic well-being. By broadening the definition of success, individuals can strive for goals that align with their values, fostering a more inclusive and diverse landscape of achievements.

3. Advocating for Systemic Change:

A significant focus of this chapter is on advocating for systemic change in financial structures. Addressing the challenges faced by black women in accessing capital is pivotal. It involves dismantling biases within financial institutions, promoting diversity in leadership, and creating policies that ensure equitable opportunities for all. Case studies and success stories are highlighted to illustrate the positive impact of such systemic changes.

4. The Role of Education in Shaping Inclusive Wealth:

Education emerges as a powerful tool in shaping the future of inclusive wealth. The chapter explores the importance of integrating financial literacy into educational curricula, starting from early childhood. It emphasizes the role of educational institutions, governments, and communities in fostering a culture where individuals are equipped with the knowledge and skills to make informed financial decisions.

5. Entrepreneurship as a Catalyst for Change:

Entrepreneurship is presented as a catalyst for positive change. The chapter showcases stories of entrepreneurs who have not only built successful businesses but have also contributed to societal well-being. Strategies for fostering an entrepreneurial ecosystem that encourages diversity and inclusivity are discussed, emphasizing the need for mentorship programs and resources tailored to support underrepresented groups.

6. Building Bridges Across Industries:

Creating a future of inclusive wealth requires collaboration across industries. The chapter explores ways in which businesses, government entities, and non-profit organizations can collaborate to address social and economic challenges. Initiatives that bridge gaps between sectors, fostering innovation and inclusivity, are highlighted as essential for creating a more interconnected and supportive environment.

7. Incorporating Ethical Considerations in Investment:

Readers are encouraged to consider the ethical implications of their investments. The chapter explores the growing trend of Environmental, Social, and Governance (ESG) investing, emphasizing the power of individuals to influence positive change through conscious investment choices. Practical steps for aligning investment portfolios with personal values are provided, empowering readers to contribute to a more sustainable and responsible future.

8. Technology as a Force for Inclusion:

The transformative role of technology in shaping the future of finance is explored in depth. From democratizing access to financial services to creating innovative solutions for inclusive wealth creation, technology is presented as a force for positive change. Case studies and emerging trends in fintech are discussed to inspire readers to embrace technological advancements in their financial journey.

9. Mindful Money Management for Generations to Come:

The final section of the chapter emphasizes the importance of passing down not just wealth but also values and financial wisdom to future generations. Strategies for instilling financial literacy, responsibility, and a mindful approach to money in children and young adults are discussed. The goal is to create a legacy of informed and empowered individuals who contribute to a future of inclusive wealth.

10. Embracing a Culture of Gratitude and Giving Back:

The chapter concludes by emphasizing the significance of gratitude and giving back as integral components of inclusive wealth. It encourages readers to cultivate a mindset of appreciation for their achievements and to actively contribute to the well-being of others. By fostering a culture of gratitude and philanthropy, individuals can play a part in building a more compassionate and interconnected world.

In essence, Chapter 15 serves as a roadmap for readers to actively participate in the creation of a future where wealth is not just a measure of financial success but a reflection of shared prosperity, diversity, and inclusivity. By advocating for systemic change, embracing education, entrepreneurship, ethical investment, and technology, and fostering a culture of gratitude, readers can contribute to a transformative shift in the landscape of wealth creation—one that is inclusive, sustainable, and empowering for generations to come.

Chapter 16

Navigating Cultural Nuances in Wealth Management

Section 1: The Influence of Culture on Money Values

Culture shapes our values, beliefs, and behaviors, and money is no exception. Different cultures may have distinct perspectives on wealth, spending, and saving. For instance, some cultures may prioritize communal well-being over individual wealth accumulation, while others may place a strong emphasis on personal success and financial independence.

In this section, we explore how cultural values influence individuals' attitudes toward money. From the role of family and community to the significance of societal expectations, readers gain an understanding of the multifaceted ways in which culture shapes money values. Real-life examples and case studies provide concrete illustrations of how cultural nuances play out in financial decision-making.

Section 2: Strategies for Bridging Cultural Gaps

Navigating cultural differences in wealth management requires a nuanced approach. In this section, we offer practical strategies for individuals to bridge cultural gaps and make financial decisions that respect diverse values.

These strategies include:

Cultural Competence: Developing cultural competence involves educating oneself about different cultural norms and values. This section provides resources and guidance on how individuals can enhance their cultural competence to make more informed financial decisions.
Open Communication: Effective communication is key to understanding and respecting cultural differences. This section explores ways to foster open and respectful conversations about money within families, communities, and workplaces.

Additionally, advocacy for inclusivity in financial institutions and policies is discussed as a means to address systemic challenges faced by individuals from diverse cultural backgrounds.

Conclusion:

As we conclude this exploration of cultural nuances in wealth management, the overarching message is clear: to build a more inclusive and culturally sensitive approach to wealth creation, we must first understand and respect the diverse values that shape financial decisions. Navigating cultural nuances is not only a personal journey but also a societal imperative for creating financial systems that cater to the richness of human diversity. By embracing these insights and strategies, readers can embark on a path toward more informed and culturally sensitive wealth management.

Chapter 17

Technology and the Future of Finance"

Introduction:

In the ever changing world of finance, technology is a major factor in how people manage and increase their money. This chapter examines how technology is revolutionizing wealth management by looking at major developments, trends, and their implications for building a more accessible and inclusive financial future.

Section 1: The Rise of Fintech

The financial technology, or fintech, revolution has disrupted traditional banking and investment models. Fintech companies leverage cutting-edge technology to provide financial services more efficiently, often with a user-centric approach. From mobile banking apps to robo-advisors, fintech has democratized access to financial tools, enabling individuals to make informed decisions about their money. The chapter delves into specific fintech innovations, such as peer-to-peer lending platforms, blockchain, and decentralized finance (DeFi), highlighting their impact on wealth creation and distribution.

Section 2: Blockchain and Cryptocurrencies

One of the most revolutionary aspects of modern finance is the advent of blockchain technology and cryptocurrencies. Blockchain, the decentralized and distributed ledger system, has the potential to transform how financial transactions are conducted, enhancing security, transparency, and efficiency. Cryptocurrencies like Bitcoin and Ethereum introduce new opportunities and challenges in wealth management. This section explores the fundamentals of blockchain, its applications beyond cryptocurrencies, and the implications of digital currencies on the future of finance.

Section 3: Robo-Advisors and Algorithmic Trading

The rise of robo-advisors and algorithmic trading has reshaped investment strategies. These technologies use algorithms and artificial intelligence to analyze market trends, optimize portfolios, and execute trades. The chapter examines how robo-advisors make wealth management more accessible, cost-effective, and tailored to individual financial goals. It also discusses the potential risks and ethical considerations associated with algorithmic trading, emphasizing the importance of responsible and transparent use of these technologies.

Section 4: Financial Inclusion through Technology

Technology has the power to bridge gaps and make financial services more inclusive. This section explores how innovative technologies are addressing financial inclusion challenges globally. Mobile banking, digital wallets, and microfinance platforms empower individuals in underserved communities, providing them with tools to save, invest, and build wealth. The chapter highlights success stories of financial inclusion through technology, illustrating how these advancements contribute to reducing inequalities in access to financial resources.

Section 5: Challenges and Ethical Considerations

While technology brings unprecedented opportunities, it also presents c hallenges and ethical considerations. This section discusses issues such as data privacy, cybersecurity threats, and the potential for algorithmic bias. It emphasizes the importance of regulatory frameworks that balance innovation with consumer protection. Additionally, the chapter explores the ethical responsibilities of technology developers, financial institutions, and policymakers in ensuring that technological advancements benefit society as a whole.

Section 6: The Future of Wealth Management

Looking ahead, the chapter speculates on the future of wealth management in the context of advancing technologies. Quantum computing, artificial intelligence, and the Internet of Things are poised to further revolutionize how individuals interact with their finances. The discussion includes the potential impact of these technologies on risk management, personalized financial advice, and the overall efficiency of wealth management processes. The chapter concludes by encouraging readers to stay informed and adapt to the evolving technological landscape to make the most of future financial opportunities.

Conclusion:

"Technology and the Future of Finance" provides a comprehensive exploration of how technological advancements are shaping the way individuals manage and grow their wealth. From the rise of fintech to the transformative potential of blockchain and the ethical considerations associated with algorithmic trading, this chapter equips readers with insights into the dynamic intersection of technology and finance. By understanding these trends, individuals can navigate the evolving landscape of wealth management with confidence and adaptability.

Chapter 18

Global Perspectives on Wealth Inequality

In the interconnected world of the 21st century, the issue of wealth inequality extends far beyond national borders. This chapter delves into the global panorama of wealth distribution, exploring the root causes, implications, and potential solutions to the vast disparities that persist across countries and continents. As we dissect the complex web of factors contributing to global wealth inequality, we aim to inspire a collective understanding and commitment to creating a more equitable and inclusive financial landscape.

Understanding the Global Wealth Landscape:

To comprehend the gravity of global wealth inequality, it's crucial to examine key metrics and trends. The distribution of wealth is often measured by metrics such as the Gini coefficient, which quantifies the degree of inequality within a particular nation or region. However, these metrics only scratch the surface of the multifaceted issue that extends across socioeconomic, political, and historical dimensions.

Socioeconomic Factors:

Socioeconomic factors play a pivotal role in perpetuating global wealth disparities. Educational opportunities, access to healthcare, and employment prospects contribute significantly to an individual's ability to accumulate and maintain wealth. Disparities in these fundamental aspects create a cycle of disadvantage that can span generations, reinforcing existing inequalities.

Political Dynamics:

The influence of political systems and governance structures cannot be overstated in discussions about global wealth inequality. Corruption, weak institutions, and policies that favor the elite contribute to the concentration of wealth in the hands of a few. This chapter explores case studies from various regions, highlighting the impact of political decisions on economic disparities.

Historical Context:

A nuanced understanding of global wealth inequality requires an examination of historical factors that have shaped current socioeconomic landscapes. Colonial legacies, historical injustices, and the exploitation of resources in the Global South by colonial powers have lasting effects on wealth distribution. Acknowledging and addressing these historical injustices is essential for creating a fairer global economic system.

Implications of Global Wealth Inequality:

The repercussions of global wealth inequality extend beyond economic concerns. Social unrest, political instability, and threats to global security are often intertwined with disparities in wealth. The chapter explores real-world examples of nations grappling with the consequences of extreme wealth gaps, emphasizing the urgent need for comprehensive solutions.

Potential Solutions and Collaborative Initiatives:

Addressing global wealth inequality requires a multifaceted approach that involves governments, businesses, and individuals. The chapter examines successful initiatives and collaborative efforts aimed at reducing global wealth gaps. It emphasizes the importance of sustainable development goals, responsible business practices, and international cooperation in creating a more equitable world.

Sustainable Development Goals (SDGs):

The United Nations' SDGs provide a comprehensive framework for addressing global challenges, including poverty and inequality. This section discusses how the SDGs serve as a guide for nations to implement policies that promote economic growth while ensuring inclusivity and environmental sustainability.

Responsible Business Practices:

Corporations play a pivotal role in shaping the global economic landscape. This section explores the concept of Corporate Social Responsibility (CSR) and how businesses can contribute to reducing wealth inequality by adopting ethical practices, fair labor standards, and sustainable supply chains.

International Cooperation:

Solving global issues requires collaboration on an international scale. The chapter highlights successful examples of countries working together to address wealth inequality, such as joint initiatives, trade agreements, and efforts to combat tax evasion on a global level.

Empowering Marginalized Communities:

A key aspect of addressing global wealth inequality is empowering marginalized communities. This section explores programs and initiatives that focus on providing education, healthcare, and economic opportunities to those who have historically been excluded from the benefits of economic growth.

Advocacy for Systemic Change:

Beyond individual and corporate actions, the chapter advocates for systemic changes in global economic structures. This involves addressing issues such as tax havens, financial transparency, and reforming international financial institutions to ensure they contribute to equitable development.

Conclusion:

In conclusion, Chapter 18 provides a comprehensive exploration of global wealth inequality, unraveling the interconnected factors that contribute to this pervasive issue. By understanding the socioeconomic, political, and historical dimensions of wealth disparities, readers gain insights into the complex challenges and potential solutions. The chapter emphasizes the need for a collective effort, involving governments, businesses, and individuals, to create a more equitable and inclusive global economy. Through responsible practices, international cooperation, and a commitment to empowering marginalized communities, we can strive towards a future where wealth is shared more equitably, fostering sustainable development and a brighter future for all.

Chapter 19

Environmental, Social, and Governance (ESG) Investing

Environmental, social, and governance (ESG) factors have seen a revolutionary change in the traditional investing landscape in an era characterized by heightened awareness of societal and environmental concerns. Chapter 19 of "Wealth Mindset Unveiled" delves into the complex world of environmentally conscious investment and highlights how important it is to the direction wealth management is taking.

The Rise of Ethical Investing

Understanding ESG Principles:

ESG investing represents a departure from conventional approaches by integrating environmental, social, and governance factors into investment decisions. Environmental considerations evaluate a company's impact on the planet, including its carbon footprint and resource usage. Social factors encompass a company's relationships with its employees, customers, and communities. Governance pertains to the company's internal structure, board composition, and adherence to ethical business practices.

A Response to Global Challenges:

The urgency of addressing global challenges, such as climate change, social inequality, and corporate misconduct, has propelled ESG investing to the forefront. Investors are increasingly recognizing the interconnectedness of financial success and positive contributions to society and the environment.

Aligning Financial Goals with Social Responsibility

The Evolution of Investor Values:

As societal values evolve, investors are seeking opportunities to align their financial goals with broader social responsibility. Chapter 19 explores the motivations behind this shift, emphasizing the desire for a more ethical and sustainable approach to wealth creation.

Positive Impact Investing:

ESG investing goes beyond risk mitigation; it actively seeks opportunities to generate positive impact. Investors can support companies that prioritize sustainable practices, social responsibility, and ethical governance. This proactive approach empowers investors to contribute to positive change while achieving financial returns.

Strategies for Effective ESG Investing

Robust Due Diligence:

Integration into Portfolio Management:

Integrating ESG principles into portfolio management involves aligning investment strategies with ethical considerations. The chapter explores how investors can diversify their portfolios with companies that demonstrate a commitment to sustainability and ethical practices while maintaining financial performance.

Challenges and Opportunities in ESG Investing:

Overcoming Greenwashing:

The term "greenwashing" refers to companies that falsely claim to be environmentally friendly. Chapter 19 delves into the challenges investors face in discerning genuine commitment to ESG principles. It provides insights into recognizing authentic ESG practices and avoiding investments that merely pay lip service to sustainability.

Industry-Specific Considerations:

Different industries face unique ESG challenges. For instance, a technology company may be evaluated on data privacy and ethical use of artificial intelligence, while a manufacturing company may be scrutinized for its environmental impact. The chapter explores industry-specific considerations to guide investors in making nuanced ESG decisions.

The Future of ESG Investing:

Regulatory Landscape:

The regulatory environment is evolving to accommodate the growing importance of ESG factors. Chapter 19 discusses current and potential future regulations, providing readers with an understanding of the legal frameworks shaping the ESG investing landscape.

Innovation and Collaboration:

The chapter explores how innovation and collaboration are driving advancements in ESG investing. From sustainable finance products to collaborative initiatives that address global challenges, the financial industry is witnessing a paradigm shift towards a more sustainable and responsible future.

Real-Life Success Stories:

Profiles of ESG Champions:

To inspire and educate, Chapter 19 includes profiles of companies and individuals who have successfully embraced ESG principles. These stories showcase how organizations can thrive financially while making a positive impact on the environment and society.

Case Studies in Ethical Wealth Creation:

Through case studies, readers gain practical insights into the financial success stories of those who have incorporated ESG principles into their investment strategies. These examples illustrate the tangible benefits of ethical wealth creation and the positive ripple effects on both investors and the world.

Conclusion: Embracing Ethical Wealth Creation:

In closing, Chapter 19 highlights how investing in ESG may have a transformative effect. Investors can help create a more sustainable and just future by coordinating financial objectives with social, environmental, and governance factors. In order to create wealth and have a significant, good impact on the world, the chapter exhorts readers to adopt the principles of ESG investment.

"Wealth Mindset Unveiled Chapter 19 is essentially a thorough guide to comprehending and managing the world of ESG investment. It encourages a new era of financial success that puts both profit and social effect first by enabling readers to make decisions that are informed and consistent with their principles.

Chapter 20

Mindful Money Management for Future Generations

In light of the impending dawn of a new era, prudent money management is more important than ever for reasons other than personal financial prosperity. The chapter "Wealth Mindset Unveiled" delves into the need of transferring money with intention, emphasizing not just material possessions but also the inculcation of moral principles and accountability in the next generation. For those who want to leave a lasting legacy that is worth more than money, this chapter offers advice.

Understanding the Legacy

Legacy, in the context of wealth management, goes beyond the mere transfer of financial assets. It encompasses the values, principles, and knowledge that individuals pass down to their heirs. By recognizing the broader scope of legacy, individuals can shape the narrative of their family's financial journey, ensuring that it aligns with their vision for a purposeful and impactful future.

Instilling Financial Literacy

One of the foundational elements of mindful money management is the cultivation of financial literacy in the next generation. This involves equipping heirs with the knowledge and skills necessary to navigate the complexities of personal finance, investments, and wealth preservation. Financial literacy empowers individuals to make informed decisions, fostering a sense of independence and responsibility.

Strategies for Teaching Financial Literacy

Start Early: Introducing financial concepts from an early age allows children to develop a foundational understanding of money.

Practical Experience: Providing opportunities for hands-on experience, such as budgeting exercises and investment simulations, enhances practical financial skills.

Open Communication: Creating a space for open and honest discussions about money reduces stigma and encourages a healthy approach to financial matters.

Fostering Values and Responsibility

Mindful money management extends beyond the quantitative aspects of wealth. It involves instilling values such as integrity, empathy, and social responsibility. By fostering a sense of responsibility for the broader community, individuals can contribute to a more compassionate and equitable society.

Aligning Wealth with Values

Philanthropy: Encouraging a culture of giving back to society instills a sense of social responsibility and contributes to positive social impact.

Ethical Investing: Introducing heirs to ethical investment practices aligns financial decisions with values, promoting sustainability and responsible business practices.

Cultivating Empathy: Engaging in charitable activities and volunteering fosters empathy, teaching heirs the importance of using wealth to make a positive difference in the lives of others.

The Emotional Aspect of Wealth Transfer

The transfer of wealth is not only a logistical process but also an emotional journey for both the giver and the receiver. Understanding and navigating the emotional nuances of wealth transfer is crucial for maintaining family harmony and ensuring a smooth transition.

Facilitating Open Family Discussions

Creating a space for open dialogue within the family allows for the expression of concerns, expectations, and aspirations related to wealth transfer. Establishing a sense of trust and transparency builds a strong foundation for successful wealth transition.

Professional Guidance

Engaging the services of financial advisors, estate planners, and family counselors can provide invaluable support during the wealth transfer process. These professionals can help facilitate family discussions, address emotional concerns, and ensure that the transfer aligns with the family's long-term goals.

Balancing Independence and Support

Encouraging heirs to pursue their passions and goals while providing a safety net of support strikes a delicate balance. This approach fosters independence and self-reliance while acknowledging the importance of a family safety net during challenging times.

Creating Opportunities for Personal Development

Investing in the education and personal development of heirs empowers them to explore their interests and contribute meaningfully to society. Providing avenues for pursuing education, entrepreneurship, or philanthropy allows heirs to find their purpose within the framework of family values.

Technology and the Future of Wealth Transfer

In the digital age, technology plays a pivotal role in wealth management and transfer. Leveraging technological tools can streamline the process, enhance security, and provide efficient ways to communicate and manage assets.

Digital Estate Planning

The digital realm is an integral part of modern life, and estate planning must extend to encompass digital assets. This includes considerations for passwords, social media accounts, cryptocurrency holdings, and other digital properties. Ensuring that heirs have access to and understanding of these digital assets is crucial for a comprehensive wealth transfer strategy.

Utilizing Fintech Solutions

Financial technology (fintech) solutions offer innovative ways to manage and transfer wealth. From digital wallets to blockchain-based smart contracts, fintech provides secure and efficient methods for handling financial transactions and preserving wealth for future generations.

Cybersecurity and Privacy

As technology advances, so do the risks associated with cybersecurity and privacy. Protecting family wealth from digital threats requires a proactive approach, including the implementation of robust cybersecurity measures, regular audits, and education on safe online practices for all family members.

Building a Lasting Legacy

Ultimately, mindful money management for future generations is about building a lasting legacy that extends beyond financial prosperity. It involves creating a narrative of success, responsibility, and positive impact that resonates through time.

Documenting Family Stories

Recording and preserving family stories, experiences, and lessons learned ensures that the legacy is not just about numbers but about the collective wisdom and unique journey of the family. This documentation can be passed down through generations, fostering a sense of continuity and connection.

Establishing Family Values and Traditions

Defining and upholding family values creates a framework for decision-making and behavior. Establishing traditions that reflect these values reinforces the family's identity and provides a sense of continuity for future generations.

Continual Adaptation

The financial landscape, along with societal norms and values, is ever-evolving. Mindful money management requires a commitment to continual adaptation. This involves regularly reassessing financial strategies, updating estate plans, and ensuring that the family's approach to wealth aligns with current realities and future aspirations.

Conclusion

Chapter 20 of "Wealth Mindset Unveiled" serves as a comprehensive guide to mindful money management for future generations. By emphasizing the importance of financial literacy, values, responsible wealth transfer, and leveraging technology, this chapter equips readers with the tools and insights needed to create a lasting legacy that transcends monetary wealth. In the end, mindful money management is not just about the accumulation of wealth; it's about using wealth as a force for positive change, both within the family and in the broader community.

www.ingramcontent.com/pod-product-compliance
Lightning Source LLC
Chambersburg PA
CBHW072341290526
45794CB00002B/965